Old TOWNHEAD'S A GONER

by

Andrew Stuart

The offices of St. Rollox Co-operative Society were situated in Lister Street, so named after the eminent physician, Joseph Lister, who initiated antiseptic surgery at the Royal Infirmary in August 1865. The street was formerly North Oswald Street until about 1920.

St. Rollox was also the title of the parliamentary seat for this area and is a corruption of St. Roche whose name was given to the chapel built around here in 1508 by Thomas Murehead, Canon of Glasgow.

© Copyright Andrew Stuart 1994
First Published in the United Kingdom, 1994, Reprinted, 2004
By Stenlake Publishing Ltd., 54-58 Mill Square, Catrine, Ayrshire. KA5 6RD
Telephone: 01290 551122
website: www.stenlake.co.uk

ISBN 1-872074-53-7

Bell o'the Brae, High Street, Glasgow, looking North.

The Bell O' the Brae was the description of the stretch of High Street from George Street to the Rottenrow and the Drygate. According to legend, it was here in 1297 that the revered Scottish patriot, Sir William Wallace, enticed the English garrison troops from the Bishop's Castle to engage into a battle and the Scottish force annihilated them.

At one time the Mercat Cross stood in the High Street at the junction of the Rottenrow and the Drygate.

In 1990 a plaque was placed on the southwest corner of Burrell's Lane to commemorate the site of one of Glasgow's earliest places of entertainment, known as Burrel's Hall.

An Edwardian postcard scene of an open-top tramcar rounding the bend of Castle Street into High Street and about to pass the gates of Duke Street Prison.

Hereabouts another ambush took place in the early afternoon of Wednesday 4th May 1921. A police van was conveying two prisoners from the Central Court to the jail when the 'Black Maria' came under fire from Irish Republican terrorists. They immediately killed Police Inspector Robert Johnston and wounded Detective Sergeant George Stirton. Several shots hit the wall and these bullet holes can still be fingered today in the remains.

In the foreground are two crenelated towers which were part of the Hydraulic Pumping Station erected in 1895 at the western top of the High Street. This Scots baronial styled building housed the pumps which supplied high pressure water for industrial purposes to premises requiring it for their hydraulic machinery.

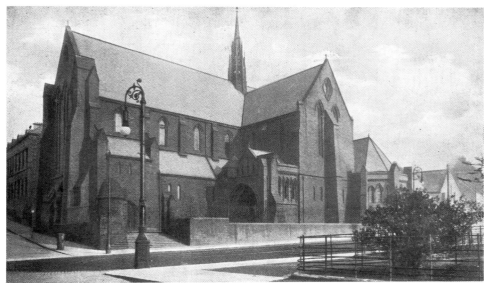

Since the reformation three congregations have worshipped in Glasgow Cathedral. The first was that of the Cathedral and was known as the Inner High. Another was the Laigh Kirk which became the Barony when they built a church for themselves. Lastly was the Outer High which, upon removal, was known as St. Paul's. Their last church at 72 John Street (right) was built in 1907. The congregation united in June 1953 with St. David's Ramshorn in Ingram Street, and both these churches were purchased by the University of Strathclyde. St. Paul's was converted into their Chaplaincy Centre, and the Ramshorn into their Drama Theatre.

The Barony (above) located at Castle Street and the Rottenrow, was built in 1886-90 and in 1984 was another University take-over. After a massive restoration programme it re-opened in 1991 as their Great Hall for installations, graduations and concerts.

All the congregations of the churches have now returned to worshipping in the Cathedral.

This delightful looking church of 1878-80 was designed by the Glasgow born architect, John Honeyman (1831-1914), who was also responsible for other handsome edifices in this city. The church is particularly enhanced by statues of the Evangelists, Matthew, Mark, Luke and John and in niches above the main doors are figures representing the Apostles, St. Peter and St. Paul. The church has had three distinct congregations during its existence — firstly the Anti-Burghers who sold their Havannah Street property to the North British Railway Company, the second was the Barony North who moved in 1941 when their church was destroyed by fire and the present congregation is that of the Glasgow Evangelical Church, who have contributed greatly to the maintenance of this building.

Castle Street, Oldest House in Glasgow.

The oldest surviving house in Glasgow is the late 15th Century Provand's Lordship. According to the 3rd Statistical Account, its proper name was the Preceptor's House of Saint Nicholas' Hospital and since 1884 the position of Preceptor has been held ex-officio by the Lord Provost.

During part of the 19th Century, this house was an inn which displayed a large sign illustrating the Bell o' the Brae Battle. Provand's Lordship is now one of Glasgow's museums and much of the furniture and artifacts were acquired by the Provand's Lordship Society, (founded in 1900), who gifted these and the property to the city.

This was the original Royal Infirmary building designed by Robert and James Adam in 1791, with the foundation stone being laid on 18th May 1792 and attended by the biggest crowd the city had ever seen at that time. The hospital opened for patients in December 1794 and during the 19th Century other buildings were added from time to time.

Some remarkable advances in medical history happened within the Royal. Doctor Robert Perry first distinguished typhoid from typhus fever, Lord Lister introduced and developed antiseptic surgery, Sir William McEwan pioneered brain surgery, whilst Matron Strong inaugurated teaching procedures for nurses.

In the Edwardian era, a new building programme was introduced to the designs of the architect James Miller and the demolition of the Adam's building as well as the Lister surgical ward, were executed.

Bailie James A. Jeffrey, in addition to his civic duties, was the Sunday School Superintendent of the Black Street Mission. In the period between the two World Wars, he arranged for Sunday Schools and youth organisations to take part in an annual Flower Procession during a Sunday afternoon in the month of June. The parade's route was from Sauchiehall Street, into Parliamentary Road and Castle Street and ended at Cathedral Square, where the children handed in flowers and fruit to the Matron and staff of the Royal Infirmary. Thousands of citizens crowded the pavements as the colourful pageant of youth passed along, accompanied by a score of pipe, brass and silver bands. A collection in aid of the Infirmary was taken among the spectators who lined the route.

Ladywell Street branches off Wishart Street and once led on to Duke Street. Within this thoroughfare were houses, workshops, a church and a "ragged" school. The street was named after the Lady Well situated in a niche on the northside wall, just below the Necropolis slope. This in time contaminated the water and caused the well to be closed to the public in 1820.

The Lady Well was rebuilt in 1874 by the Merchants' House of Glasgow and a plaque at the side indicates that it was renovated in 1983 by Tennent's breweries. This old established firm has taken over almost all of this area, and in another extension in the early part of this century, they occupied the Wellpark Church which is now incorporated within their workshops.

The City Council's housing scheme built on the site of Duke Street Prison in the early sixties and the old Alexander's School, built in 1858, are both named "Ladywell".

THE OLDEST THATCHED HOUSE IN GLASGOW   BRANDON SERIES.

According to legend, the slope from Duke Street down Ladywell Street was once known as the 'hangman's brae' and, residing in this thatched house, was the public hangman. This Edwardian postcard depicts part of the house as a coal depot whilst the rest is up for sale. To the extreme right is the edge of an advertisement for the "Glasgow Hippodrome Theatre, adjoining the Zoo, in the New City Road, the best place for amusement in the City".

Today the offices of Tennent Caledonian Brewery cover all this scene.

11

CASTLE ST & BLIND ASYLUM.
GLASGOW

Royal Asylum for the Blind Brass Band, 100 Castle St., Glasgow.   Band Master—R. M'Donald.   Terms on application to Band Secy.   [Copyright.

The architect for the Royal Blind Asylum (1879), was William Landless, a cousin of a more eminent Glasgow architect Sir John J. Burnet, who designed the nearby Barony Church of 1886. (see page 5). The Asylum's steeple is distinctive, being six-sided with a clock face on four of them. There is also a statue, sculptured by Charles Grassby, representing Christ welcoming a little child into his midst.

The Blind Brass Band often paraded in the streets, being guided by partially sighted bandsmen and others by means of decorative cords attached to everyone.

The building became the Infirmary's Dispensary in 1940, but is now in disuse. The Health Board have indicated that they won't be too difficult in settling a purchase price for the "B" listed steeple. It may be beneficial if they could dismantle that ugly wooden canopy, which was erected many years ago.

The shape of things to come can be seen by the elevated motorway cutting across Townhead. By the early seventies, the buildings in Stirling Road and the western side of Castle Street had been demolished to make way for roadways, which would have also resulted in the destruction of the Martyrs' School, had not the New Glasgow Society and the Charles Rennie Mackintosh Society rallied public opinion against this upheaval.

The Fountain was to be re-sited south of the river but again the outcry determined the transfer to the nearby road junction of St. James' and Stirling Road.

The fittings around the public convenience, such as the railings and the decorative gas lamp-post, manufactured by Walter MacFarlane's Saracen Foundry, seem to have disappeared completely.

Alexandra Parade was named in honour of HRH the Princess of Wales who later became HM Queen Alexandra when HM King Edward VII ascended to the throne.

The Parade began at the Townhead, as depicted here, and ended about a mile beyond at the junction to Cumbernauld Road in Dennistoun. From the mid-fifties, part of it was nicknamed Tobacco Road because of the cigarette factories and warehouses of Stephen Mitchell (pre-war). Will's Imperial Tobacco Company and Gallacher's, all of which have now ceased to operate. Also gone in this scene of the Parade are the two streets on the right – Glenfield and James Orr.

The tenement at the corner of Castle Street/Parson Street and opposite the entry into Alexandra Parade, had the words "Townhead Cross" sculptured upon it. This was the most serious traffic jam within the district and commuters could be delayed by over a half hour on their journey homewards during the evening "rush" hours, a problem "resolved" by demolishing everything shown in this 1958 scene. New roadways eased the traffic on to the M8 motorway in the seventies and, upon part of the cleared areas, new wing extensions were built for the Royal Infirmary. Pedestrians were not forgotten either, for they could ignore at their peril the footbridges and underpasses supplied for their convenience.

James Graham, proprietor of a few cinemas in Glasgow, commissioned the building of the Carlton Picture House in 1925. At that time he published privately a book entitled "Martyrs' Monument" by Thomas M. Weir which explained the history of the monument and its re-siting into the cinema's wall. Unfortunately this is hidden behind the blue tramcar turning into Monkland Street on the No.6 route from Alexandra Park to Scotstoun.

On Tuesdays and Fridays children scampered out of schools to join the queue awaiting entry into the cinema for a penny. This was known locally as the "Penny Rush" but by the amount of kids admitted, it could equally have been called the "Penny Crush".

Facing the Carlton was another picture palace of an earlier date called the Casino. It was once owned by that man of property A.E. Pickard, the eccentric millionaire. This house entertained audiences with a mixture of silent films and variety acts of local talent until the "talkies" took over. The sheltered canopy and the side alcove were greatly appreciated by the inevitable queue of patrons on stormy nights. Good use was also made of Hilley's the ice cream shop next door. During the intermissions, an usher would parade the aisles with ice cream wafers for sale, the forerunner to the choc-ices and squash drinks of a later era.

Townhead Library (which can be seen behind the No.32 tramcar) is the only remaining building hereabouts and is now unused and boarded up. A slip road on to the M8 is at its southside whilst landscaped gardening and a bus shelter adorn the north.

The library opened on 4th July 1907, the architect being John Fairweather, and upon its completion, a £100,000 donation, given in 1901 to the Corporation of Glasgow by Andrew Carnegie for the building of city libraries, was exhausted. He immediately granted further money for the building of Possilpark and Langside libraries.

The steeple of the former Blind Asylum and the towers of the Royal Infirmary are the only existing landmarks in this 1955 scene of Castle Street at the junction of Royston Road, formerly known as Garngad and still referred to by the locals in rhyming slang as the "Good an' Bad". Trolley buses were on regular service via Royston Road to Riddrie and tramcars continued to serve Springburn folk. When the canal was filled in, these roadways were re-aligned and both the tramcars and trolley buses ceased as public transport here in 1959 and 1966 respectively. Buses now service these routes, but be warned, be patient!

This scene of Royston Road at the Castle Street end, shows on the right hand side the railings surrounding the children's playground with its robust equipment of swings, maypoles and roundabouts, now a football pitch for St. Roch's Secondary School. In front of the Charles Street high rise flats is the small housing scheme of Royston Square, built in 1919 on the site of a disused cotton mill. This scheme was the first to be built by Glasgow Corporation and a sun-dial plaque on one of the houses commemorated this event.

One of the original tenants was James Maxton, the beloved MP for Bridgeton from 1922 to 1946.

Miss Hamilton's class of '34 assembled for their photograph at the girls' entrance of St. Rollox School, now known as Royston Primary. The boy nearest to the teacher was Winston Spencer Churchill, whose family firm manufactured prams and prospered in the baby boom after the Second World War. Charlie Rodgers (back row) was the tallest in the class and grew up to be tall in the saddle as well – he retired as a constable in the Royal Canadian Mounted Police.

ST. MUNGO F.C.

St. Mungo FC was possibly the district's most successful club in the minor leagues, although supporters of Germiston Star, Provanside Hibs or Townhead United might disagree. They started as a street team from Villiers Street in the Garngad and their home pitch was at Glenconner Park, gifted to the community by the Tennants of St. Rollox Chemical Works.

Their keenest rival was Huntingdon FC from Springburn and old timers can still recall their 'needle' matches of the thirties.

The players in this 1936-37 season's team are: T. Etterson, A. Watt, G. McGovern, T. Mooney (Captain), R. Adams, E. Mutter, H. Nelson, D. Neilson, R. Muroy, J. Barr, W. Blakely.

St. Roch's Junior Football Club play at Provanmill Park, Royston Road, and at the junction of Broomfield Road. They were formed in 1920 and became the Division Two Champions in that season. In the next one, 1921-22, they were the Champions of Division One and the winners of the Scottish Junior Cup. No mean feat, and definitely helped by their goal scoring centre forward, who became one of the great legendary heroes of the Scottish Football League – "Jimmy McGrory", the famous player and manager of Glasgow Celtic.

In this line-up of the players of the 1936-37 season are: C. Reid (Captain), A. Docharty, J. Murray, W. Devlin, J. Sommerville, T. Brawley, T. Loughran, E. Brady, H. Scougal, H. Bradley, C. Sharky.

Garngad's steamie was in Garnock Street and this shows the interior with the stalls, washing machines, benches and the heated drying compartments. Pre-booking with payment by the hour was necessary for the use of this equipment and the housewife had to supply her own soap powder and washing board (which later became an essential part of skiffle groups). To convey the clothes to and from the wash-house, she would use an old pram or a zinc bath, mounted on a bogie frame.

Townhead's other steamie was in Kennedy Street and passers-by would often see the firemen stoking up the boiler furnaces. To be the talk of the steamie, incidentally, was not considered a compliment.

The Steel Company of Scotland had two steelworks – one at Hallside Newton in Lanarkshire and the other was Blochairn in the north side of Glasgow.

Blochairn manufactured steel plates of various lengths and thicknesses for engineering and shipbuilding firms. They also produced steel tyres for locomotive engines and wagons. Latterly they were taken over by Colvilles which eventually became part of British Steel and Blochairn was closed down in the subsequent reorganisation.

The main entrance was in Blochairn Road and was attended by the Corp of Commissionaires. The other entrance was for workmen only who crossed the canal by bridge near the top of Sannox Gardens in Dennistoun.

The traffic has been given the green light to continue into Springburn and beyond having just crossed the bridge over the canal which was known as the "Cut of Junction". This was the link between the Monkland Canal at Townhead Basin and the Forth and Clyde basin at Port Dundas.

In 1799, Charles Tennant and his cronies established the St. Rollox Chemical Works on the northern bank of the 'Cut' and manufactured bleaching powder, soap and sulphuric acid. Within two generations, the works became the largest of this kind in Europe. The entrance and offices can be seen at the left.

When St. Rollox works were on full production in the 1840s, 120 tons of coal were consumed daily. The smoke, combined with gases emitting from the chemicals in use, made it necessary to erect a structure to dispel the fumes. Professor William McQuorn Rankine of Glasgow University designed a 435ft chimney which became the principal landmark of this district from 1842 and was proudly referred to as "Tennant's Stalk".

Long after the chimney became disused, work was undertaken gradually and with great care to reduce the height to 280ft. In March 1922, the structure had become dangerous and eight men were engaged on its demolition when the edifice suddenly gave way in the late afternoon of Friday 10th March. Four of the men were killed instantly and three others were seriously injured. All the squad resided in the south side and were employed by John Cumming of Rutherglen.

These two draperies of the early twenties show the standard style for displaying clothes, each clearly priced, and crammed into their windows as well as hanging above the doorways.

The shop of John Inglis was in Castle Street, next door to the district's chemists of McCowan and Adam, who had the three traditional coloured bottles and stone jars in one of their windows. Inglis later became a gentleman's outfitters, Hunter Tomlinson, which disappeared in the redevelopment.

Margaret Baird's shop was in Garngad Road and vanished during earlier changes made for new housing and shops.

The Townhead Floral Bazaar belonged to Mrs Agnes Brogan who is seen here with her family and staff posing outside the shop-front in Castle Street. Many bridal parties purchased their bouquets and buttonhole flowers here. Mourners could also order wreaths and crosses as well as ornamental shells, small marble tablets and flower containers with the words, "Sadly Missed" or "Deepest Sympathy" imprinted upon them.

The store also sold fruit and vegetables, especially those man-daft potatoes advertised at $2^1/2$d per quarter stone. Children often received a bargain bag of chipped fruit for a penny.

The firm of Agnes Brogan is still flourishing in George Street and is renowned as a top-class florist and Interflora agent in Glasgow's Merchant City area.

Starting off as McGregor and McCaffer circa 1890, this business eventually ended with the McCaffer family solely in charge. Their shop-sign of a gilded horse was best seen from the top of a tramcar entering Parliamentary Road. Their windows were packed with horse collars, harnesses, reins and all the stable requisites needed for those hard working Clydesdales to haul the goods loaded on carts throughout the city. Both horses and carters worked six days per week in all kinds of weather.

McCaffer's workshops extended through to Monkland Street and were very industrious before the coming of the automobile era.

This was the spot where the traffic from Springburn and Provanmill converged with that from Dennistoun to head into the city centre and beyond.

Nearby were the Unionist Rooms which were used for political and social gatherings and were also hired out regularly by their leftwing opponents for Trade Union meetings.

The MacDonald Arms was typical of Parley Road's many pubs. It was the idle boast of the 'macho' man or the hardman as he was described in these bygone days that he could drink in every bar – 'a hauf an' a hauf' – (a $1/4$ gill of whisky and a half pint of beer), and would still be standing at the end of the road. Saturday night's drunks proved that many didn't make it.

Lindsay's was a typical grocer's shop and was located in Parliamentary Road just beyond Martyr Street. A large staff was necessary as many provisions had to be handled and weighed. Ham or bacon would be sliced thick or thin to the customer's wishes, butter would be patted and wrapped in grease-proof paper, cheese was cut by wire, sugar was scooped from sacks and biscuits selected from tins. (No broken ones please, would be the instructions). The costs would be totalled up mentally or on a scrap of paper and if a pound note was tendered, change-back would be expected. It must be stated, however, that the wages of a working man would amount to single figures in those bygone days.

Thompson's was in Parliamentary Road near Glebe Street and was patronised by the housewives of Townhead searching for an attractive and fashionable garment, be this a coat, costume or a frock for that special social occasion such as a wedding, works' dance or a church soiree.

In the days before television addiction, many women would hold knitting and sewing bees in each other's homes and the Hosiery Manufacturing Company's shop would be their calling station for patterns and materials. Next door was Malcolm Campbell, whose fruit and vegetable stores were scattered throughout Glasgow.

Possibly the most popular shop of all, was at the other end of the fruiterer's. This was William W. Watt, Parliamentary Road's main butchers, whose back entrance in Taylor Street can be seen in this picture. Even before the Second World War, queues of eager customers lined up to purchase Watt's famed sausages, steak pies and prime Scotch beef.

Co-incidentally, the city centre branches of Watt and Campbell were beside each other in Renfield Street.

The shops, in the background between Ward and Lister Streets, were the main stores of St. Rollox Co-operative Society.

Between Lister and Drummond Streets were numerous shops and one of longevity was Smith's Paint and Wallpaper Co. Ltd., located beside the pole supporting the tramway wires. Its bollard would probably be manufactured in the nearby Sun Foundry of George Smith in Kennedy Street.

The hatter, James McCulloch, had two windows chockful of shirts and collars which required attachment by front and back studs plus a lot of patience. The other window was stacked with workmen's cloth caps, or as Glaswegians prefer to call these – "bunnets!"

The unusual steeple was that of the McLeod Memorial Church located at the corner of Parliamentary Road and Murray Street. In 1944 the congregation joined with the Barony and the McLeod building became a Youth Centre until 1967, when the Corporation compulsarily acquired the premises for demolition.

The billboard partly obscured by the tramcar was one of two which fronted the Grafton Picture House. This was once workmen's lodgings called St. Rollox Home. Another cinema conversion was that of St. James which consisted of the first landing accommodation of a tenement in Stirling Road. Known locally as the "Buggy" their programmes were altered every Monday, Wednesday and Friday instead of the twice weekly changes of the three other Townhead cinemas.

David Rattray started his business in Edwardian times at Murray Street, as an agent for cycles and accessories and sported an authentic penny-farthing bicycle as his shop sign. He also manufactured his own cycle frame, "The Flying Scot" in his workshop and these were eagerly sought by members of local racing clubs.

In 1950 the business expanded into the premises as depicted and these were compulsarily purchased by the Corporation of Glasgow for the urban redevelopment planning of the seventies.

In the other photograph, the chap with the pipe was the World's Sprint Champion, Reg Harris of Manchester Wheelers. Two of the others and wearing dustcoats were Mr. Jack Smith, the manager who became the proprietor upon the death of the founder and his right hand-man, Jack Potter, the longest serving employee of the company.

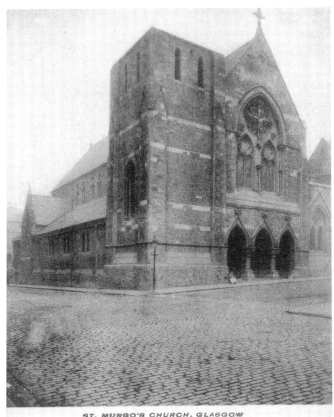

ST. MUNGO'S CHURCH, GLASGOW.

ST. MUNGO'S GLASGOW.

The parish of Saint Mungo, Townhead, did not exist until 1850 so Catholics of the district had no other option but to walk to Saint Andrew's Cathedral in (Great) Clyde Street, or to Saint Alphonsus' in Great Hamilton Street, (now London Road), if they wished to attend Sunday Mass. Their chapel was not completed until 1869 and is in the French Gothic style, designed by George Goldie. Next to this is the Saint Mungo's Retreat. (1892 by Father Osmond Cooke), the residence of the parish priests and the Marist Brothers, who were the conductors of teaching to the boys of Saint Mungo's Academy, which was adjoined to these buildings.

The Academy was the only casualty in the redevelopment and a new one was built in 1972-7 in the Gallowgate, next to the Crown-point Sports Centre.

In September 1970, Martin Donoghue photographed these pupils from his old school, Saint Mungo's Academy. No doubt their menu was less enticing than the pies and cakes bought from the local dairy in Parson Street, and there were a few other shops hereabouts. Felix O'Connor had two shoe repair shops. A most unusual business was at the corner of Martyr Street. This was Carruth's Grotto, a religious repository which sold statues, bibles, pictures, communion dresses, capes and suits. They removed to the south corner of Castle Street and Alexandra Parade, and then to premises opposite the casualty entrance of the Royal Infirmary. This firm is still in business and has a shop in the High Street, next to Bow's Emporium.

In 1537 Jerome Russell, a Greyfriars Monk, and John Kennedy, a student from Ayr, were burnt to death for adhering to their beliefs in the Reformation cause. Their execution was near to the Cathedral and it was in their honour that this church, built in 1838, was called "The Martyrs". The location was in Monkland Street, and the street nearby, as well as the Martyrs' School, erected in 1895 to the designs of Charles Rennie Mackintosh, were also to their memory. Only the school has survived the upheaval of the M8 motorway.

A new church was built in Saint Mungo Avenue to house the congregation and was dedicated for worship on 9th September 1977.

This Martyrs' School Football Club in the 1919-20 season has a broth of a boy in the front row centre as their goal-keeper, who grew up to play in the same position for Greenock Morton FC. However, he was more renowned in the Scottish Football Association circles as a first-class referee, who lived up to his name – Charlie Faultless!

Sitting cross-legged at the left is the father of the author whose eldest son, John, was a "dead-ringer" of his grand-father at the same age.

McAslin Street originally started at St. James Road and finished at the far end in this postcard view. The short stretch into Parliamentary Road was once called Catherine Street and had the Catholic Apostolic Church (1852-1970) at the corner. In the early twenties, this wee street became part of McAslin, which also was extended eastwards to Martyr Street, taking in what was Albert Street in that city-wide renaming period.

The name was derived from the long established seedsmen, Austin and McAslan who had their nurseries hereabouts, and the misspelling was one of a few such occurrences. A few years ago, when the nearby North Frederick Street had its nameplates renewed, the maker designated this as Fredrick, but fortunately this blunder was promptly corrected.

Behind the northbound tramcar were the administrative offices for the London, Midland & Scottish Railway Company and towards the town were the stables for the same company for their door to door deliveries.

In the early part of the 19th Century this contained the Lunatic Asylum and their gardens from 1814 to 1841 until Gartnavel came into use. 322 Parliamentary Road then became the City Poorhouse until shortly before being demolished in 1908.

New administrative offices were built for British Railways on the site of the old Buchanan Street Station, Port Dundas Road, and were called Buchanan House, now ScotRail House.

HOLMHEAD ST GLASGOW 229 G.M

Holmhead Street stretched from North Frederick Street to Dundas Street but may be better remembered as Cunningham Street when name changes were carried out by the Glasgow Corporation in 1922 to avoid duplication and confusion. The railway bridge, built in the 1880s when Queen Street Station was extended is all that exists today. The entry from North Hanover Street is closed and is a landscaped slope, whilst the Dundas Street end is part of a make-shift car park, almost in front of the new Glasgow Royal Concert Hall. The church on the left was the Dundas Congregational and another on the opposite side was the Tron St. Mary.

44

This convoy, coming to the end of Parliamentary Road, consisted of two steam traction engines hauling a low-loader laden with a Springburn built locomotive for the Egyptian State Railways. They would be preceded by two police motor cyclists clearing the journey to the big crane at Stobcross Quay. In days of full employment, every four out of five locos built in Glasgow would be exported and some are still steaming somewhere in the world

Although the tenements have long since been turned into rubble, no use has been found for the eyesore vacant site in nearly twenty years.

Dundas Place was part of a five way junction where Buchanan Street intersected with Cathedral and Bath Streets. At the other end, Dundas Place joined onto Dundas Street, just above Queen Street railway station. There was a tea-room and baker's shop in the little inshot at the end of the lefthand building in this view. Above their window was a metal place which had inscribed upon it "Here stood the old thorn tree terminating the Garscube Trust 1827".

At the end of the other side was the Koh-I-Noor restaurant and bar which was a favourite howff of the late Jack House. This became the Dog-House in the 1950's until the bulldozers arrived. (See inside front cover).

ENTRANCE MATERNITY
HOSPITAL, GLASGOW

RELIABLE SERIES

Many Glaswegians have passed through these gateways in one way or another, with some knowing that this is officially the Glasgow Royal Maternity Hospital, but still refer to this place as 'The Rottenrow' or 'The Maternity'. The present building was designed by R.A. Bryden in 1903 and completed by 1906, with parts of an earlier one of 1880 still surviving.

However, if the present plans to build new maternity blocks within the precincts of the nearby Royal Infirmary succeed, then the redundant buildings or sites will most certainly be utilised by the ever-encroaching University of Strathclyde, which has territorially taken over almost all of the southside of Townhead.

By the will of Allan Glen, a Glasgow wright, a good practical education was to be freely given to some 50 boys, mainly sons of tradesmen and artisans. This institution was established in 1853. Allan Glen's, shown here at the corner of Cathedral Street and North Hanover Street, ceased free education in the mid 1870s and was managed by the Governors of the Glasgow and West of Scotland Technical College, (now the University of Strathclyde), and gained a reputation as one of the foremost "Science Schools" in Britain.

In 1912, Allan Glen's was transferred to the Glasgow School Board and was closed down as a fee-paying school by Glasgow City Council about 1980.

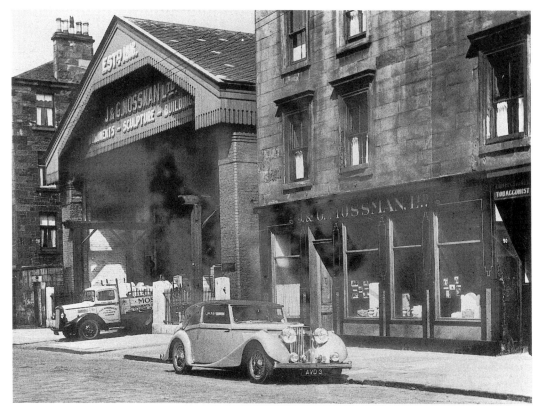

Many statues, and most of the sculptures on Glasgow's buildings erected during the latter half of the 19th Century, were the works of one family – John, George and William Mossman. The best testimonies to their name were the sculptured figures for the St. Andrew Halls. All of these survived the disastrous fire and now adorn the frontage of the Mitchell Theatre in Granville Street.

The monumental sculptors yard was once in Mason Street (now Cathedral Street), and many of their tombstones and memorials can be seen in the Necropolis and in local cemeteries. On the site of these works today is the car park for patrons of the Clydesdale Bank.

After the death of John Mossman in 1890, his foreman, Peter White, acquired the business which has survived and can be located in the High Street.

The building with the tower is that of Wm. Collins, Sons & Co. Glasgow. The founder started as a printer in 1819 and soon started to publish religious and educational books. In 1842 he received a licence to publish his first edition of the Bible, which became the mainstay of this family business. When he died in 1853, he left a prosperous and expanding firm, whose works were in St. James Road and Taylor Street. The main offices were at 144 Cathedral Street. His son, Sir William Collins, was the Lord Provost of Glasgow from 1877 to 1880 and in the following year a fountain was erected by the Temperance Reformers in recognition of the valuable services rendered to the cause by Sir William. This monument was placed outside the Glasgow Green entrance, opposite to the Judiciary Courts, but has now been re-sited inside the park.

HRH Princess Margaret, accompanied by the Right Honourable Bruce Millan, Secretary of State for Scotland, as on her way by State Coach to Glasgow Cathedral to join HM Queen Elizabeth and HRH Duke of Edinburgh in the Silver Jubilee National Service of Thanksgiving in 1977.

They are about to pass the building which was the Collins company's extension and was completed earlier in that decade. When this publishing business transferred to Bishopbriggs, both this building and the remains of the older one were refaced in brick and became part of Strathclyde University as the Curran building, the Andersonian Library and the University book-shop.

This aerial view of the late sixties centres on the Royal Infirmary and Glasgow Cathedral. At the top left is the Necropolis with Tennent's Wellpark brewery in the centre whilst to the right is the Great Eastern Hotel and the Ladywell housing estate. At the bottom left only the steeple and the facade of the Royal Blind Asylum remain. Glebe Street and Stirling Road are now part of new roadways and St. James Road has been partly landscaped and partly utilised for car parking.